Curious George®

Takes a Trip

Adaptation by Rotem Moscovich
Based on the TV series teleplay
written by Raye Lankford

Houghton Mifflin Company
Boston 2007

For information about permission to reproduce selections from this book, write to Permissions, Houghton Mifflin Company, 215 Park Avenue South, New York, New York 10003.

Library of Congress Cataloging-in-Publication Data
    Moscovich, Rotem.
    Curious George takes a trip / adaptation by Rotem Moscovich.
    p. cm.
    "Based on the TV series teleplay written by Raye Lankford."
    ISBN-13: 978-0-618-88403-2 (pbk. : alk. paper)
    ISBN-10: 0-618-88403-3 (pbk. : alk. paper)
    I. Lankford, Raye. II. Curious George (Television program) III. Title.
    PZ7.M8494Cut 2007
    [Fic]—dc22
                                    2006101786

Design by Joyce White

www.houghtonmifflinbooks.com

Manufactured in Singapore
TWP 10 9 8 7 6 5 4

Winter was long, cold, and snowy
in the big city.
George and the man with the
yellow hat were lucky . . .

They were going on vacation!
The suitcases were ready.
The tickets were ready.

George and his friend went to bed early.
Everything was set . . .

except the alarm clock!

"George! We overslept!" the man cried.

George and his friend dressed.

They dashed off to the airport.

"Hawaii, here we come!" the man said.

George was excited.

He had never been on an airplane before.

The man put the suitcases on a cart at
the airport.
"This will make them easier to carry,"
he said.

They rushed
to check in.
George climbed on top of the cart to
see over the ticket counter.

"Here is a gift for you," the ticket
clerk said.

She gave George a toy plane.

His first airplane!

George liked the airport already.
He flew his plane.
It landed on a red suitcase.

"Bad news," the man said.
"Our plane is late because of a big storm.
We have to sit and wait."
George did not mind waiting.

He had a brand-new toy.
But when George looked,
the toy was GONE!
The suitcase was gone!

Then George heard a beeping sound.

A motor cart drove by.

The red suitcase sat on top.

George ran after it.

The suitcase went faster.

George got on the moving sidewalk.

But he was going the wrong way!

George heard a new noise.

Bags were moving on a long belt.

George spotted the red suitcase.

It was getting away.

George followed it.

He looked inside the suitcase.

No toy plane here.

Where should he look next?

Finally, the plane was ready.

But where was George?

"I cannot board the plane," the man said.

"I lost my monkey!"

"You mean George?"
the flight attendant asked.
She pointed at the plane.
George waved. He was on board already.

George and the man walked to their seats.

A nice woman stopped them.

"There you are! Did you lose this?" she said.

She gave George his toy plane.

That airport was a fun place!
There were so many different ways
to get around.
Maybe it was even better than vacation.

TRAVELING
Things and people get around in different ways.

Match the object or person with its mode of transportation.

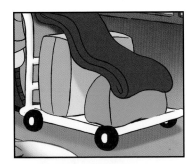

ON THE GO!

Balloon-Powered Train/Car:

You will need safety scissors, tape, a straw, a toy car or train, and a balloon.

1. Cut off the lip of the deflated balloon.
2. Cut the straw in half. Stick the straw into the balloon and tape it in place. Be sure to make a tight seal.
3. Tape the straw to the top of a car or train so the straw extends off the end.
4. Blow up the balloon using the straw and seal the balloon by pinching the straw's end.
5. Set the car down on a smooth surface and let it go.

Getting There Is Half the Fun

A great way to take your own trip is to draw your destination and a "road map" to get there on a piece of butcher

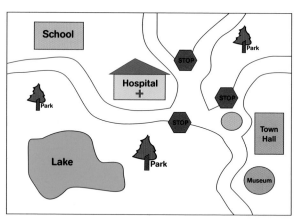

paper. Tear off a section as long as your table. Draw roads, buildings, and street signs. Now you can play with your small cars on your extra-large map!